Democratic

Book of Strategy

Learn more at
www.NBCnews.com

Thornberg Books
Phoenix, Arizona 85013

ISBN-13: 978-1519634962
ISBN-10: 151963496X

Table of Contents

Introduction	1
The Economy	17
National Security	33
Education	49
~~Islamic Terrorism~~, Domestic Violence	65
~~Abortion~~, Women's Health	81
~~Global Cooling~~, ~~Global Warming~~, Climate Change	97
Social Security	113
Healthcare	129
Deleting Emails	145
Minimum Wage	161
Veteran Affairs	177
Taxes & The IRS	193

Introduction

Why This Book is Needed

Chapter 1

The Economy

Chapter 2

National Security

Chapter 3

Education

Chapter 4

~~Islamic Terrorism~~, Domestic Violence

Chapter 5

~~Abortion~~, Women's Health

Chapter 6

~~Global Cooling~~, ~~Global Warming~~, Climate Change

Chapter 7

Social Security

Chapter 8

Healthcare

Chapter 9

Deleting Emails

Chapter 10

Minimum Wage

Chapter 11

Veteran Affairs

Chapter 12

Taxes & The IRS

www.ingramcontent.com/pod-product-compliance
Lightning Source LLC
Chambersburg PA
CBHW071342280526
45787CB00001B/187
9781519634962